Harmony Enterprises presents

TIE DYE, BACK BY POPULAR DEMAND

By Virginia Gleser

Harmony Enterprises

MODESTO, CA   209-571-2767

The loving relationship that my husband, Robert, and I have shared for twenty-four years has been the foundation of all of my creative endeavors. When my tie-dye business outgrew the garage, he built me a studio. When we outgrew that, he built a larger one. He's in charge of marketing, editing, remodeling, washing machine repair, vehicle maintenance, and taking out the trash as well as running his own business. Somehow he found time for his most important endeavor, raising our six children. His devotion to our family has been my inspiration. To him, I dedicate this book.

ISBN 0-9647247-0-7 (pbk.)

Table of Contents

ACKNOWLEDGMENTS

Many people have helped me in writing this book and I wish to thank everyone for their support and encouragement. Our customers' and patrons' interest and avid enthusiasm has been the inspiration for this book. Many have become part of our extended family.

The craft show family of artists is a constant source of strength and community. The craft fair promoters, who put on such wonderful shows are especially appreciated.

Thanks to my parents, Paul and Sophie Crane, and my sister, Tish Rainey, for helping us with the editing. Linda Rake, Stacy Kerr, Kristan Levin and Terry McGuffin have also helped with the editing and have been close friends for many years.

Don Schneider has done a wonderful job of photographing my work, insisting on good results. He is an artist of photography and photographing my artwork was a challenge to which he skillfully rose. Thanks also to Gowans Printing Co.

I want to thank Rhonda Chapman, Sia Lo, Elaine Wright, Bla Thao, Roshni Naidu, Susie Chang, Fay Hendrickson and many others for their skillful help and artistic camaraderie.

My six children, Brian, Eugene, Saul, Audrey, Rosie and Olivia, are not only inspirational, but became part of our business as well. They would get up at ungodly hours to do shows with us and gave up many weekends and summer weeks. They immersed themselves in the endeavor with a sense of humor and their wonderful energy and interest. They helped make hard work and long hours into a good time.

INTRODUCTION

At every craft show (53 in l994), we are asked "How do you do tie-dye?" Usually the requests are from school aged kids, accompanied by their supportive parents wanting to do a "cool" project. For the last twelve years our response to this request has been to sell the PRO Chemical and Dye Company dye kits.(See Sources). These kits feature procion dyes and a brief introduction to dyeing. Along with the kit we also warned parents that tie-dyeing can be quite a production. Most things that come in contact with the dyes get stained (actually dyed), including plastic containers, floors, clothing and skin. Everyone should wear rubber gloves whenever handling dyes, and use a dust mask when mixing dye powder.   This warning usually discourages some people, but those who stick with it take their dye kits home and "do their thing."   Many return wanting to know more: more ties, more dyeing techniques, more...,but, show time is not really the time or the place to give instructions. Now, comes the book to answer questions about tie-dyeing and help the budding artist along.

3

ABOUT THE AUTHOR

In l950, when North Korea invaded the South, my missionary parents evacuated to Osaka, Japan, where I was born. We returned to our home in South Korea in l953, where I was raised with many oriental influences.

The Korean people dress their children in bright primary colors, and when I was young, my Korean dress was a bright red and green, with rainbow colored stripes on the sleeves. When I was in elementary school in Seoul, I had the opportunity to take dance lessons from a famous Korean traditional dance teacher. The costumes we wore were full length, beautifully colored dresses. The keen sense of color that is a part of Korean and Japanese culture has inspired me throughout my life. (See color picture 7-D).

As a girl, I always wanted to be an artist like my grandmother, Florence Hedelston Crane, who was known for her floral and landscape watercolors. My favorite childhood memories were of visiting my grandmother. She would let me paint with her "palette of one hundred colors," taught me how to mix colors create shadows and draw in perspective. I also learned about artistic license, where an artist can alter and balance a picture to look right, even though it isn't exactly how it appears in reality. She never went anywhere without her sketch pad, and always returned home from a trip with new material to paint.

I moved to the United States to attend college at the age of seventeen. There I studied art, my favorite project being a batik picture. I spent many nights working in the studio to create a multi-colored design with five different overlays of wax and dyes.

In the winter of l969 I moved to San Francisco, California. The anti-war movement was going strong, and the hippie experience was evolving from dancing in the streets and taking drugs, to the commune scene. A large group of young people were trying to figure out if this new lifestyle could make living feel more relevant. Could we survive, raise children and create a community with some of our idealistic beliefs in tact? Could we exist in peace with each other and our environment? People gathered every Monday night at an old ballroom called the Family Dog near the beach in San Francisco. Discussions florished about every facet of life. Stephen Gaskin, who had been a professor at San Francisco State College, was the leader of the meetings and would steer the dialogue so that our many questions could be raised and answers explored.

Stephen was invited on a lecture tour around the country to various colleges and churches. He was going to adjourn the "Monday Night Class." However many people from the class wanted to go with him to carry the message of peace and love across the country. On Columbus Day, 1970, about 200 people in 70 buses and vans started out on a new discovery of America.

My husband Robert and I, with some other people who wanted to go on this adventure, fixed up an old bus and joined the caravan. The trip took us across the West. At one of our stops in Yellowstone National Park, I received a vision that would later shape my life. Standing alone under the clear starry night sky, I saw that I was one of a group of Native American women weaving cloth of many beautiful colors and intricate designs. At the time I was wearing a brightly colored skirt woven in Native American patterns and I realized that I was connected to this land. As an artist, I would honor the Great Spirit. I kept this vision close to my heart, even though it took many years to manifest into reality.

The caravan wandered across the United States visiting New York, Philadelphia and Washington D. C., headed south and west by way of Atlanta, Nashville and Tulsa, finally returning to California. By the time we reached the Pacific, many more people and vehicles had joined our group. It had been a peaceful and exciting trip, but it was over. What were we going to do now? Along the way, we had grown close and had emerged as a tribe or a "village on wheels." People helped each other: those who had money paid for gas and food. There were mechanics who fixed the buses and there were midwives who delivered the babies. Nobody wanted to break up and go separate ways. We pooled our resources, boarded our buses and vans once more and moved across the country to settle in rural Tennessee. There these 21st century pioneers bought some land and founded the intentional spiritual community called The Farm. For the next twelve years, Robert and I lived the great hippie experiment and began raising our six children.

In 1978 we moved to Miami, Florida to help with Plenty, the Farm's world relief program. Plenty had projects in Guatemala, Africa, the Caribbean, and Native American lands of South Dakota. In Miami we took care of the physically challenged and senior citizens. We also supported a forty member crew in Guatemala which helped rebuild a town destroyed by the 1976 earthquake. The project helped bring water to the village and set up a soy dairy.

While we were living in Florida several women got together in the evenings and had tie-dye parties. We tie-dyed our families' clothes as well as household items. We had fun sharing our knowledge and trying new designs and folds and color combinations. The children loved the next day when we untied and opened our work. It was like opening presents at Christmastime.

When we ran out of old clothes to experiment with, we bought new t-shirts to work our magic on. We gave them as gifts to friends and relatives. Then friends of friends started asking if they could have tie-dyed t-shirts too. We decided to start making some for sale. A friend of mine, Lori Young, and I asked our husbands if they would watch the children one day a week so we could dye without our two year olds getting their fingers into the dyes. At that time, the men were roofing subcontractors. We promised them that we would make enough money for them to take the day off. They were skeptical but gave us a chance. We tied the shirts during our kids' nap times twice a week and built up a batch to dye on Wednesdays. The men would take the kids to the beach, the park, or the science museum and we would dye our hearts out. We enjoyed our work and loved the next day when we would open the shirts up and "ooh" and "aah" over the new designs we had created. During our critique sessions, we would talk over changes in color and design. For example: the spiral needed to be placed higher so it was not centered over the belly butto, the orange was too strong, the yellow was swallowed up by the blue, the red wasn't squeezed in enough, and so on. The artistic debate continued until we were satisfied with our art. Tie-dye is a trial and error skill. The more we tried new folds and used new color combinations, the prettier the work turned out. And they sold! This was very satisfying. We took them to some stores that would allow us to consign them. Both children's and adult stores reordered. We took our clothing to a farmer's market in Coconut Grove and sold many shirts. The income was taking up the financial slack and the guys didn't mind that. They even enjoyed doing some of the selling.

In 1983 our family left The Farm and resettled in California. We wanted a change and we left with our six children in an old station wagon with enough money to rent a house and get started again. Robert was employed immediately as a roofer, and I borrowed $60 from his early paychecks to buy a dozen T-shirts and some dye. I was in business again...this time in my garage, on my own, in California. I tied when my baby was taking her naps and the other children were in school. I would dye one day a week. Robert took the shirts to several stores. "Tie-dye is out, didn't you know, even on Haight Street in San Francisco," was the response. He asked if they would take a dozen shirts on consignment. We would come back in a month and pick them up if they hadn't sold. In two weeks they were sold out and the stores wanted more. After that we didn't have to consign them. We bought a used washing machine for $85.00 and the money I made went back into buying more dye and shirts.

That fall we signed up for an Octoberfest craft fair in a little gold rush town in the Sierra foothills called Murphys. We were so excited. The whole family went to our first craft fair in the old station wagon with a table and a few bags of tie-dyed shirts. People walked by and said, "Is that tie-dye?" or "What is that?" or "Look at the bright colors!" We came home with almost $300.00 and we were thrilled.

With our six children helping us we have built Harmony Enterprises. We purchased and remodeled some buildings in the commercial part of town and built our studio and store. Some of the kids added remodeling skills to their small-business education. More than a decade later Harmony Enterprises continues to allow me to develop my artistic skills. It's been a satisfying journey helping to establish tie-dye as a respected American art form.

TIE-DYE, BACK BY POPULAR DEMAND

Tie-dyed clothing has once again exploded onto the marketplace. At almost every festive occasion one can spot a brightly tie-dyed t-shirt in the crowd. There are tie-dye parties, projects at camp, and school art projects using tie-dye. It's fun, it's individual, it's a fashion statement, it's colorful, it's creative and it's daring. It might even please parents, who may have done some tie-dyeing themselves "in their younger years."

Bright colors are "in" these days. Men's fashions that used to be rather drab, have flourished with colorful ties and bright casual clothing. Women often put a splash of bright color with their business suits to show a little individuality. Kids love bright colors, and putting on a brightly colored outfit gives them a charge of good energy. Teens enjoy making an individual visual statement in their choice of clothing. Besides all of this, color is fun.

In many cultures, it is traditional for the peasants to dress in bright and colorful clothing. The Guatemalan Indians weave beautiful materials for their tribal costumes, each village having its own distinct colors and designs of cloth. The Gypsies of Europe wore bright swirling skirts and beautifully embroidered vests. Japanese kimonos are works of art often incorporating tie-dyed designs known as *tsujigahana*. In Bali, India and Africa, tie-dye and batik is used to brighten sarongs, saris, skirts and *dishekis*. The Seminole Indians of Florida sew colorful materials together for their native dress; it's a sign of their tribe. This use of color is their connection to a talented tradition. In these days of economic uncertainty and global friction, clothing can give relief and a healthy diversion, especially clothing that you make yourself and enjoy wearing. The American melting-pot has created its own tribal dress, with tie-dye emerging as an American crafted art form.

Some people romanticize the 1960's era as a time of idealism, peace, love and innovation. Tie-dyed clothing is seen as a symbol of those times and is being worn not only for a taste of nostalgia, but as a statement that those ideals still exist.

WHAT IS TIE-DYE

Tie-dye is just what its name implies. The clothing or material is tied and then dyed. Of course, it isn't that simple. Tie-dye is a technique of dyeing using the resist method. Resist is when something like string, rubber bands, wax, clothespins, paper clips or stitching is used to keep the dye from being absorbed into the material. This resist method creates designs and patterns depending on the placement of the resist materials. The design is also affected by the amount of dye used and where it is placed.

Batik is a cousin of tie-dye. Batik is done by painting or stamping with wax a design onto material. The dye does not penetrate the wax and the design shows through, often with interesting lines where the wax has cracked and dye has slipped in. Although this is an interesting art form as well, in this book we are going to be dealing exclusively with tie-dye.

Tie-dye requires a dyeable material which is folded, pleated, or scrunched to create different patterns and designs. These are then tied off with rubber bands or string, or sewn together so it doesn't come apart in the dyeing process. The item can then be dipped or dunked in a dye bath or vat, or dye can be squeezed or dripped onto it. When the ties are removed, the design emerges from where the ties were. A random or specific design can be created depending on how the folding and tying are done. Each part of the process allows for many possibilities and that's what makes tie-dye so varied and interesting.

A HISTORY OF TIE-DYE

Tie-dye dates back to ancient times. It was one of the ways our ancestors decorated their clothing, along with beads, shells and other ornamentation. I think back to the story in the Old Testament of the Bible, of Joseph, the son of Jacob. He had a beautiful coat of many colors that was the envy of his brothers. Could it have been tie-dyed?

Tie-dye became fully developed in China during the T'ang Dynasty (6l8-906 A.D.) and in Japan during the Nara period (552-794 A. D.). The availability of silk and hemp, which are very receptive to the resist technique, made these countries' art outstanding.

Some early tribes in Western China, South East Asia and Central America tied and dyed the threads before weaving their cloth. When it was woven into material, beautiful designs appeared where the white lines of the tie contrasted with the colored dyes. This method is known as *ikat.*

The colors in the dyes were mostly extracted from roots, flowers, leaves and berries of plants. These include the blackberry, some species of lichen, safflower, marigold, onion, red cabbage, sage, and a long list of other plants. One of the most popular dyes came from a plant called indigo that makes a beautiful blue dye and is still used today. Some people enjoy the time-consuming process of growing plants and making them into natural dyes. The one problem with these dyes is that over time and in sunlight, the colors fade.   Today, synthetic dyes have been developed that are permanent, quick-setting, easy to use, bio-degradable and the colors are ensured by accurate formulas. In this book, we will be using these synthetic dyes, but don't let this stop you from learning about natural dyes. An excellent book, A Dyer's Manual, will tell you more about this. (See Bibliography.)

As in days of long ago, we still use natural fibers for tie-dyeing. The silks from China and cottons from Egypt are still prized, as is the rayon from Bali. Knit cottons made in the United States are our staple. A hemp material made in Hungary and The Netherlands is making its appearance as a durable and dyeable natural fabric.

The tie-dye methods using cotton and silk were passed down in Japan, Indonesia, and Southeast Asia, while cotton and raffia were used in many parts of Africa. Pre-Columbian Peruvians used wool and cotton to make *ikat* designs in their weaving.

In Japan, about l200 A. D., tie-dye was a common way of decorating peasants' clothing. Each family could create a little individuality and color in their otherwise hardworking and tedious lives.

From 1568 to 1603, in what's known as the Momoyama period, *tsujigahana* reached its height. *Tsujigahana* is an art combining tie-dye with ornamental drawing using Chinese ink called *sumi*. Tie-dye may be the entire design or it can create large areas where flowers, landscapes and trees are drawn into the designs. Traditional dye shops developed new methods for making elegant silk robes.

At that time Japan was divided into kingdoms that were ruled by warlords. Fighting and raids of one warlord against another were common. The more powerful warlords slowly began taking over their weaker neighbors. Some battles were furious. When an officer of a warlord's army was particularly brave or had won a great victory, the lord would give him gifts of recognition. One of the most prized awards was a tie-dyed kimono or *kosode*. These have been passed down in some families as prized possessions and many can be found in museums throughout Japan. Over time, the various plant, root, and berry dyes have faded, but the designs of flowers and detailed misty landscapes can still be admired.

These beautiful kimonos exhibit interesting variations in the use of tie-dye. One variation was the creation of a white area by tying off a large piece of the material before dyeing the robe. Then ink would be used to draw pictures on the white area. In another design, rice would be tied into the material in little circles, so that when the material was dipped in blue dye, designs of little white circles would be scattered over the deep blue kimono.

The popularity of tie-dye and the famous dye shops lasted for three hundred years. Eventually the peasants could no longer afford to wear tie-dyed kimonos, but high-society women and their influential and wealthy husbands took pride in wearing these intricate hand-crafted pieces of artwear. The era of the powerful warlords came to an end during the seventeenth century and the tie-dyed kimono took a back seat, replaced by embroidered cloth from China. However, one can still find shops in Japan that carry on the tradition of tie-dyeing beautiful material.

In Africa ceremonial hats were decorated with tie-dye as were the caftans. In recent years, many local African women earn money for their families by tie-dyeing material for caftans, shirts and tablecloths. Many varied styles of tie-dye have emerged to distinguish the different nations of Africa.

In the U.S. during the Roaring 20's pamphlets were printed that gave directions on how to decorate homes with tie-dyed curtains and throw-pillows. We have met several senior women who have told us of making tie-dyes when they were young girls during the Great Depression of the 1930's. They would cut up cotton flour sacks, tie-dye them, and then sew them into clothing, curtains, pillow covers and tablecloths. When times are rough, tie-dye has been a way to brighten peoples' lives.

Tie-dye came back in style in the 1960's, when a great movement emerged among young people, that emphasized individuality. It was time to "do your own thing." Each person could make his or her own statement by tie-dyeing his clothes with this tie or that color combination. Tie-dyed sheets were used as room dividers and wallhangings. Silk and cotton banners were used as backdrops for rock and roll concerts.

Since the 1980's, tie-dye has come back into style. It is also slowly being recognized as a highly skilled and sometimes quite difficult and labor intensive art form and craft. Many different colors can now be put on one item to get intricate and detailed designs in brilliant colors. The dyes, which used to fade so badly, have been replaced by dyes that are permanent and easier to use. They can be in bright rainbow colors, or toned down blues, blacks and reds, and earthtones. Pastels are perfect for someone with more conservative tastes. The designs are endless.... a spiral, a star, stripes, a bulls-eye, random scrunches, a yoke, a heart, a peace sign and many more....and each one unique.

A MODERN JAPANESE TIE-DYER

When Itchiku was a young boy growing up in Japan in the 1930's, he worked as an apprentice in a dye house. He learned the ancient techniques and skills of dyeing and tie-dyeing. In Japan, the old ways were revered and apprentices had to start by learning the old ways before they were allowed to branch out and try new ideas and methods.

During World War II, Itchiku was drafted and sent to Siberia. There he was captured and held in a concentration camp for six years. He kept himself alive and sane by meditating on the beautiful and ever-changing sunsets on the cold Siberian plains. He visualized these sunsets tie-dyed on beautiful silk kimonos. When he was finally released from prison and returned home, he was able to bring his dreams into reality. Itchiku now runs a famous dye house in Japan where he produces robes of museum quality. He has done a beautiful series of five kimonos of the Siberian sunsets. They start off in brilliant oranges and reds and as the sun sets, mellow into grays and lavenders and pinks. One can visualize the cold Siberian winters and sense the hope that the colorful sunsets brought to him. Another series of five robes uses water as the theme, with beautiful designs in greens, blues and aqua.

Itchiku's tie-dye designs are created first by drawing on the silk pieces that make up the kimono. He then sews the designs along the edges and pulls them together. Sometimes a thread will go through only two strands of silk cloth. The method is tedious but the results are exquisite. After sewing the design, he vat dyes or applies the dyes onto the cloth, steams it and unties it. He then sews it again on different lines and repeats this process as many as thirty-five times per piece. This gives beautiful shadings of many colors. After the pieces are untied, the different strips of material are sewn together to make the complete kimono. One robe can take up to eight months to complete.

Itchiku's work can be seen in a lovely book called <u>Opulence</u>.

TIE-DYEING SUPPLIES NEEDED

There are several different types of dyes available for tie-dyeing. The dyes available in local grocery stores have been used for many decades. They are inexpensive, but must be used with boiling water. The results often appear faded and are not very permanent. A new dye called a "cold water fiber reactive dye" has been developed since the 1950's. This type of dye does not require hot water, and the colors are brilliant and permanent. The molecules of the dye actually combine with the molecules of the material to form a strong and permanent bond. These are the dyes that I prefer. They can be purchased at many local craft shops or can be ordered from several dye distributors around the country. We sell a beginners' starter kit from Rupert, Gibbon and Spider. (See the listings under sources). The cold water reactive dyes come under several brand names including Procion*, and Deka Dyes. Some dyes are made for tie-dyeing and batik while others are made for fabric painting. There are dyes that are more applicable to cottons and rayon while others are better for silk. Reactive dyes can only be used on natural fibers including cotton, rayon, wool, hemp and silk. For best results be sure that the items to be dyed are 100% natural. Although polyester/cotton blends can be dyed, only the cotton in the blend will take the dye and the effect will be muted. In the dyeing and rinsing process the natural fibers will shrink so when dyeing wearable items be sure to use clothes that are at least a size larger than normal. In normal cotton sheeting items the shrinkage can be as much as one inch for every six inches of material.

String, rubber bands, clothespins, needle and thread, blocks of wood, rice grains, marbles, and many other items have been used to make the designs of tie-dye. Each gives a unique and interesting effect. This is where experimentation comes in. If tying with string, any weight from kite string to dental floss can be used. If sharp contrasts between white and color in the designs is desired, a strong twine is recommended. It is always helpful to experiment.

Containers, measuring cups and spoons will be needed to made up the dye. Small plastic containers like cottage cheese or tofu containers are a good size for small amounts of dye and larger plastic containers are good for dunking large items.

Warning: The dyes are considered relatively non-toxic, but we advise using a respirator and work in a well ventilated room. Wear rubber gloves that come up as high as possible when mixing and using the dyes. The unmixed dye is a fine powder and repeated inhalation of the powder can cause an allergic reaction in some people. There is a good cleaner, Reduran, that takes dye off of the skin. Keep dye away from the eyes and mouth. Children should be closely supervised when using these dyes. Pregnant and nursing mothers need to be particularly careful with all chemicals. It would be best to discuss this matter with one's doctor before using these dyes. Once the utensils and containers have been used for dyes, they should not be used for food. With minimum precautions and common sense, a safe and enjoyable time can be had.

Applicators are necessary when applying the dye. Many dye companies and craft shops sell squeeze bottles of varying sizes that work well. Eye droppers can also be used to create special effects.

Some <u>mixing agents</u> are needed when making up the dyes. Most dye companies supply these with the dyes and have recipes for mixing the dye solution. There are many different formulas that give different results, so some experimenting will be necessary to reach the desired effect. Even the hardness or softness of the water in a particular region will cause different results, and water softener is often added or decreased to reach the desired formula. Some of the chemicals that are used to mix with the dye powders include soda ash, urea, baking soda, washing soda, and water softener. Follow the formulas that have been supplied with your dye kit.

For Example: This is the cold batch method using *Dharma Procion Dyes.*
First mix up a cold batch of chemical water which can be stored a month or more in the refrigerator. (Make sure it is sealed and labeled!)
The chemical water is made by mixing the following ingredients together:
> 1/4 cup Urea (dissolve in hot water if necessary)
> I quart water (add a little Water Softener if needed)Pour off the amount of chemical water that is needed for one color (for ease of measurement, use I cup increments.) To each cup of chemical water add:
> I tsp. Soda Ash Fixer (be sure it dissolves)
> Some thickener to thicken the liquid dye (optional)
> Add the dyes in the amount needed for each color (mix should look darker than desired since some will be washed out in the process.) Try a pre-dissolved concentrate and add water and stir until color is right.

For one cup of water add:

Shade	Pale	Medium	Dark
Dye Powder *	I tsp.	3 tsp.	6 tsp.
Soda Ash Fixer	2 tsp.	3 tsp.	4 tsp.

* For the deepest shades, some colors need to be doubled and some need to be quadrupled.

Do the above for each color that will be used. Don't mix more than is needed for one work session as the addition of the Soda Ash Fixer commences the chemical action and it begins to set. The mixture will gradually lose strength and four to six hours later will be half exhausted: the results will be faded. If this is inconvenient , there is a way around it. First pre-soak the fabric in the soda ash solution (I cup per gallon of water). Next leave the soda ash out of the dye mixture (water, urea, thickener), and then add the dye. The dye, mixed as above without the soda ash, can be saved for several weeks if refrigerated.

These dyes are bio-degradable and can be safely poured down the drain. One environmental consideration is that the soda ash in the dye bath creates akaline(high PH) liquid. By adding a little white vinegar(low PH), the acid will be neutralized. It is a good idea to neutralize the dyebath water before putting it down the drain into a septic system. PH test paper can be obtained from Dharma Trading Co.

* Procion is a trademark of ICI PLC

NOW IT'S TIME TO TIE-DYE

Read over this chapter once before beginning a tie-dye project.

Stage One: The first step in tie-dyeing is folding and tying the material. This is the essence of the art form. How the folds are made will determine how the design comes out. I have often compared my tying with the Japanese art of paper-folding called *origami.* Detailed folding of the cloth creates intricate patterns. I'm going to discuss some of the easier designs first so that everyone can try them and become familiar with the different results.

To start, decide whether to tie the item wet or dry. A wet item is easier to fold. Some formulas state to soak the cloth in soda ash solution before folding. Others say to tie the cloth dry and soak the item later. Tying cloth soaked in soda ash can be hard on the skin, so use tight gloves that give you dexterity. Surgical gloves are good for this. The right wetness is very important to the final results of the tie-dyed item. If the fabric is too wet, the dye becomes diluted and a washed-out lookwill result. If the item is too dry, the dye will not penetrate into the cloth and there will be large irregular white areas. If the items are tied dry, they can be dampened before dyeing. To test dampness squeeze the item firmly. There should be no water dripping from it.

To tie wrap the string or rubber bands around the design to secure it.

Stage 2: The next step after folding and tying is dyeing. This is the fun but messy part. It is a good idea to wear old clothes, shoes, and rubber gloves. I love this stage of the process, because here color is the medium. No more all white items! Although the dye companies can supply you with over seventy colors, I mix most of my own colors. I enjoy mixing dyes that will blend well with other colors to create an overall piece that is pleasing to the eye. Whether the dyes are used straight out of the container or mixed, the results will be exciting. Visualizing the color sequences or drawing them on paper will help one decide how to place the colors. The dye that is made up will look much darker than the final result, after the item is rinsed, so adjust the colors accordingly. They may need to be made thicker or thinner, depending on the desired results. Some colors, when put next to each other, result in a brown or muddy effect. Suppose that the holiday colors of green and red are wanted. These colors will blend into brown at the points where they meet. They must be separated by a section of white or black to make sure the colors remain clean.

Most of the items that we tie have sections tied off with string. Each of these sections can be dyed a different color or one section can be carefully dyed with several colors. The larger sections that are to remain a solid color, such as the background, can be dunked in a large container of dye, being careful to hold the tied sections of the item out of the way, so as not to get dye on them. An applicator can be used to get into creases and near the string lines. Squeeze out any excess dye so that it doesn't run up into the tied sections. It's a good idea to hold back the amount of dye used near the string line, because when it is squeezed in, the dye will "creep" more deeply into the material

Each color of dye has its ownpersonality. Red is what I call a stubborn color. It is thicker and does not flow into the material easily. The folds that are dyed red need to be checked carefully to make sure that the color has penetrated enough. Usually more dye will need to be added. Yellow is our precious color and it is easily lost or overrun by other colors. Yellow can always be covered with another color,, but once it is lost, there is no getting it back. The blue, turquoise, green, orange and black are runaway colors, so they need to be applied carefully with a little room left for them to run, because they will. Orange, a very bright color, can easily run over yellow. In a batch of amateur tie-dyes the orange is often dominant and garish, so be careful. Purple, a mix of red and blue, has some of the characteristics of both. It needs to be checked, but tends to absorb pretty well. Purple bleeds a beautiful shade of blue so it's nice to have some white left in the purple section. Knowledge of the behavior of the individual colors is essential for a balanced and pleasing piece of work.

Stage 3: After the dyeing process is finished, it is time to play the patience game. This is always the hardest part for the new artist, because it's hard to wait to see the results. There are no one-hour photo labs for tie-dye. The dyes need to set up. Cover them with plastic and set them aside to ripen for between 12 and 24 hours. This will give the most "bang" for the dye. The colors will truly be rich instead of faded and washed out.

Stage 4: Now it's time to untie and open up the dyed articles. Each one is unique and beautiful. Cut the string or rubber bands carefully so as not to cut the cloth. If possible use a scissors with one point blunted for this step.

Stage 5: Unfold the material and rinse in cold water until the water runs fairly clear. Next wash it in the hottest water possible, adding some synthropol soap (available from the dye companies) to remove the excess dye from the item. Remember, in the time the articles were sitting, the dye was combining with the fabric. What is being rinsed out is excess dye that didn't bond. If it is thoroughly rinsed now, it will not run. Add some water softener at this hot water stage so that the items stay soft. For the final rinse wash the items in a warm wash/cold rinse to remove any excess soap and dye. The water should be clear on the final rinse. Dry your beautiful creations in a regular dryer or hang them up to dry.

1-A - Diagonal Stripe, partially dyed

1-B -Diagonal Stripe, Completed

1-C - All-Over Stripe, partially dyed

1-D - Horizontal All-Over Stripe, Completed

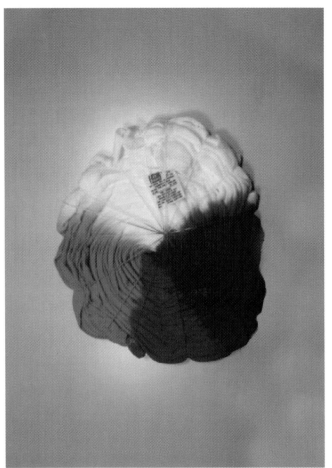

2-A - Spiral, partially dyed

2-C - Spiral, Completed

2-B - Spiral, completely dyed

3-A - Flower, partially dyed

3-C - Flower, Completed

3-B - Flower, completely dyed

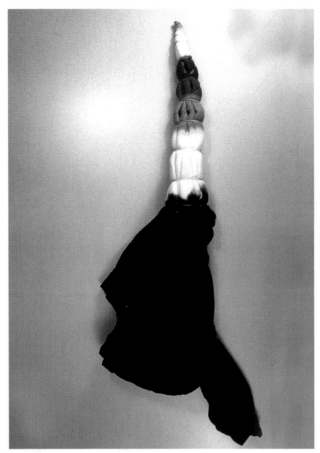

4-A - Bulls-eye, partially dyed

4-C - Bulls-eye, Completed

4-B - Bulls-eye, completely dyed

5-A - Yoke, partially dyed

5-B - Yoke, completely dyed

5-C - Yoke, Completed

6-A - Shibori, partially dyed

6-C - Shibori, Completed

6-B - Shibori, completely dyed

7-A - Spiral outfits

7-B Children's clothing-spiral and yoke designs

7-C Fawn Dot design on silk

7-D Classic Korean fan

8-A Wallhanging - Eight point mandala

8-B Shooting star and mandala yoke designs

8-C Heart design

8-D Quilt - sixteen mandalas

Designs to Try

Design #I: <u>The Accordion Fold.</u> This is one of the easiest folds, but also offers many variations. Different variations can result from how large the pleats are, how even each pleat is, and where the pleats are placed on the item. The folds can be placed diagonally, vertically, horizontally or in a zig-zag stripe. The design can cover the entire item or it can be partially tied so that a solid colored background sets off the design.

The Vertical Stripe Design

a. To fold the vertical stripe, divide the shirt in half along the diagonal from the shoulder to the opposite bottom corner of the shirt. Start folding in accordion pleats from the bottom edge of the shirt to the opposite shoulder. Try to keep the pleats small and even.

b. Secure the folds with string. Make as many sections as you wish. We made three.

c. To dye the vertical stripe, first dye the background a solid color. Try purple, red or black. Squeeze out any excess dye. Then dye the end section yellow. To guard the yellow, place a little yellow on the next section. Apply green to one half of the next section adjacent to the yellow and turquoise to the other half. The last section is blue. Over the end of the yellow section, place a small orange section and then a red section on the very end. (See color pictures IA - IB).

The Horizontal Stripe and the All-Over Stripe Designs

How to tie the horizontal stripe with a background and a horizontal stripe over the entire shirt are shown on these two pages.

a. Fold the shirt in half across the chest. At the fold pleat across the shirt from one side to the other in small, even pleats.

b. Tie the horizontal stripe in three sections or continue to tie it all the way out to the end of the material for a design that covers the entire shirt.

c. To dye the all-over stripe, squirt different colors on each section that is tied. If a rainbow design is desired, place yellow in one of the central sections. Yellow should always be used first in any design, since it is a light color and can easily be taken over by other colors near it. To guard the yellow, give it a little extra room on each of the adjacent sections. In one direction from the yellow section dye an orange section, then red, purple and blue. Many people like blue near the face while some like yellow and red near the face. Decide on the placement of the dye before starting. In the opposite direction from yellow, apply green, turquoise, blue and purple on each section in that order and a beautiful rainbow stripe will appear. If there are more sections begin the sequence again. (See color pictures IC-ID). To dye the horizontal stripe, follow the directions for the vertical stripe on the previous page. (See color pictures IA - IB).

.   **Design #2:** <u>The Spiral.</u> This is one of the most popular designs.
a. To tie the spiral, the middle of the spiral is held down while the rest of the material is swirled around the center. The middle can be secured with a finger, a stick or a fork. Again, the accordion fold is being used, but in a circular motion. The care and detail that is given to the folds will result in a more detailed spiral or a more random looking spiral. There is a tendency for the folds to get too big, so each large fold must be divided into two folds as the spiral is being pleated.   When the folding is completed, it resembles a mini pizza, or a party-size pizza if a large item is being tied.
b. Some people tie spirals with rubber bands, but there is more control over the outcome by using string. Tie the spiral securely without losing its circular shape, but not so tightly that it collapses the design.
c. To dye the spiral think of it as a pie. Each color will be a slice of pie. We will describe a rainbow spiral here, but there are an infinite number of color combinations for the spiral that can be substituted here. Again a warning when choosing colors: some will become muddy when placed next to each other. Dye a big slice of the pie yellow, a smaller slice orange, and another larger slice red to make up about half of the pie. The other half, starting next to the red, will be made up of a small purple section, a large blue one, and a smaller green wedge. We have made the primary colors (yellow, red and blue) the larger sections and the secondary colors (orange, purple and green) the smaller sections. An emphasis on primary colors will give a more balanced rainbow effect. Be very careful when applying the dyes close to the middle of the spiral, so that there will be a multi-colored center.   <u>Remember</u>: all the colors, when mixed, become black or brown. (See color pictures 2A-2C and 7A-7B).

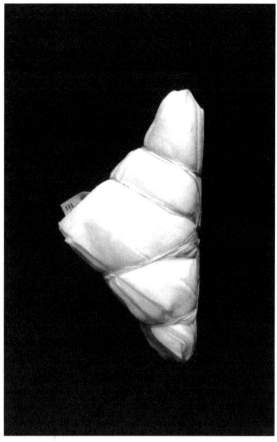

Design #3: <u>Butterfly or Flower Fold.</u>

a. In this fold, three or four vertical accordion folds are made across the entire item to create one long piece.

b. The piece is folded in the shape of a triangle and folded back and forth up the entire length of the shirt. Secure this triangle shaped piece with rubber bands or string to hold it together. This does not need to be tied too tightly, because of its thickness. The dye must be able to penetrate its many layers.

c. To dye the flower, apply yellow to the sections on each of the two similar corners. Make sure the yellow has penetrated the material. Squeeze out excess dye or blot the material with a rag. At the tips of each yellow section, apply an orange section and then a red section on top of the orange, mostly covering the orange. Remember, orange takes over anyway.

d. Above the yellow section, place a green section and then a turquoise one. The middle section toward the third corner should be blue with purple on the third corner. In this design, due to the thickness of the fold, the sections need to be checked for too much white and filled in as much as possible. Although an item tie-dyed in this style seems to be filled with dye, the resultant design will still contain a large amount of white. Blot any dripping dye with a clean rag. (See color pictures 3A-3C).

Design #4: <u>The Bulls-eye.</u> A bulls-eye is a popular design from the '60s. Create one big circle in the middle of your item or lots of little ones all over it.

a. Grasp the material where the center of the bulls-eye will be and tie it off in sections. The center can be a large section, if a ring effect is desired. If a target design is wanted, the whole bulls-eye can be tied in smaller sections as in the pictures.

b. A loosely tied item will allow more dye to penetrate the cloth. A tightly tied item will leave more white in the design.

c. To dye this design, first pick a color combination. Apply a different color in each section and squeeze it in well. Try the rainbow color sequence with a yellow center or a blue center and continue the sequence on the remaining sections: orange, red, purple, blue, and green. If a ring effect is desired, dye the large center section the same color as the background color, with different colors on the tied sections, or leave the tied sections white. (See color pictures 4A-4C).

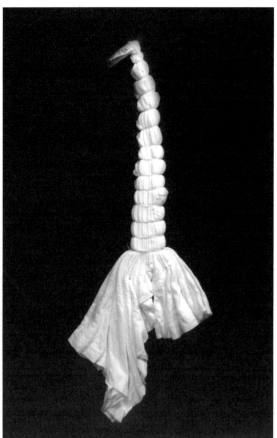

Design #5: <u>The Yoke.</u> A yoke design is like a necklace. This design can be a shallow necklace or a deep V-shaped design.

a. Fold the shirt in half vertically from the middle of the collar to the middle of the bottom of the shirt.

b. Decide if a deep or shallow yoke is desired. Pick a place on the fold of the shirt and pleat it from this spot to outside the sleeve seam.

c. Tie off sections of the yoke in one inch or two inch sections.

d. Dye the background or untied section of this design first. Dip it carefully in a tub of dye, holding the tied design up and away from the dye. It helps to have two people for this step. One can hold the tied design and one can dunk the background.

e. Squeeze in the dye. Lift the shirt out of the dye and squeeze out the excess dye.

f. The yoke design can be dyed like the stripe or bulls-eye. If ithe rainbow sequence is desired, start by putting yellow in the middle section. (See color pictures 5A-5C and 7-B).

Design #6: <u>Shibori.</u> This is a Japanese method of tie-dyeing that gives a flowing zebra-striped effect.

a. The Japanese use bamboo. We use wooden dowels or a PVC pipe. Wrap the material around the wood on a diagonal.

b. Scrunch the material up to one end of the wood.

c. Wrap string around and around the material to secure it there.

d. Submerge the wood with the material tied on it into a tub of dye (or dye can be applied to the material with squeeze bottles).

e. After the material has been dunked in the dye and set, untie and rinse. The process can be repeated to add one or more colors. This over-dyeing effect makes for beautiful and unplanned results. The shibori method gives an attractive flair to scarves and pieces of cloth that can later be sewn into clothing. (See color pictures 6A-6C).

Design #7. <u>Fawn-Spot Method.</u> Another way of tying used by the Japanese is called the "fawn-spot" dyeing method.

a. Small dotted circles are made by wrapping pinches of cloth at the base with twine, or sewing, before it is immersed in the dye bath.

b. Rice grains can also be sewn into the material in a design or a random pattern. Marbles or other objects can be used to make bigger circles. This is a tedious process if many circles are desired, but it is very intricate and the results are fantastic. (See picture 7C). This is an example of Japanese fawn-spot from an antique silk kimono. Notice the spot where the tie came undone during the dye process.

Color Pictures 8A-8D. This page features the heart, the mandala, the shooting star and the combined design called the mandala yoke. These designs are quite difficult and will be featured in our next book, coming out soon.

Conclusion

The designs described above are a few ideas on which to begin. Let your imagination take it from here! Some of these designs can be combined. The inner artist in all of us takes over and creates original patterns and methods.

After the pieces of art are completed, the job of art critic comes into play. This is the time to really see what has been created, what is pleasing, and what needs improvement. How did the designs turn out, the placement of color, the color sequence? To be a serious artist and improve your techniques, take notes for the next tie-dye session. Otherwise it is easy to forget what to change and what to keep the same. By doing this, the work will show great improvement and there will be much satisfaction in mastering this complicated and intricate art form. The fascinating thing about tie-dye is that each piece comes out unique and individual. The public is beginning to become aware of the skill needed to tie-dye and will appreciate any effort.

I hope this book has provided many enjoyable experiences creating tie-dyed artwear, and furnished an understanding of the intricacy and finesse of this art form.

Sources for dye:

Dharma Trading Co.
PO Box l50916
San Rafael, Ca. 94915
l-800-542-5227

PRO Chemical and Dye Co.
PO Box l4
Somerset, Mass. 02726
l-508-676-3838

Rupert, Gibbon and Spider, Inc.
PO Box 425
Healdsburg, Ca. 95440
l-800-442-0455

Bibliography

Fiber Arts Supplies Catalog, Dharma Trading Co., San Rafael, Ca. 1994.

Fabric Vibrations, Tie and Fold-Dye Wall Hangings and Environments, Museum of Contemporary Crafts of the American Crafts Council, New York, 1972.

Goodwin, Jill, A Dyers Manual, Palham Books, London, 1982.

Shaw, Robin and Jennifer, Batik, New Look at an Ancient Art, Doubleday and Co., Inc., New York, 1974.

Toshiko Ito, Tsujigahana, The Flower of Japanese Textile Art, Kodansha International Ltd., Tokyo, Japan, 1981.

Edited by Tomoyuki Yamanobe, Opulence, the Kimonos and Robes of Itchiku Kubota, Kodansha International USA Ltd., New York, 1984.

NOTES